DIRT BIKES

by
Lori Polydoros

Consultant:
Dirck J. Edge
Editor
MotorcycleDaily.com

CAPSTONE PRESS
a capstone imprint

Edge Books are published by Capstone Press,
151 Good Counsel Drive, P.O. Box 669, Mankato, Minnesota 56002.
www.capstonepress.com

Printed in the United States of America in Stevens Point, Wisconsin.
092009
005619WZS10

 Books published by Capstone Press are manufactured with paper
containing at least 10 percent post-consumer waste.

Library of Congress Cataloging-in-Publication Data
Polydoros, Lori, 1968–
    Dirt bikes / by Lori Polydoros.
    p. cm. — (Edge books. Full throttle)
    Summary: "Discusses the history of dirt bikes, their design, and the events
dirt bikes are used in, including motocross and freestyle competitions" — Provided
by publisher.
    Includes bibliographical references and index.
    ISBN 978-1-4296-3940-8 (lib. bdg.)
    1. Trail bikes — Juvenile literature. I. Title.
TL441.P65 2010
629.227'5 — dc22   2009022120

Editorial Credits
Carrie Braulick Sheely, editor; Tracy Davies, designer; Jo Miller, media researcher;
    Laura Manthe, production specialist

Photo Credits
Alamy/Stephen Bardens, 4, 5, 19, 23 (top); AP Images/Jeff Roberson, 14;
AP Images/Phil Sandlin, 15; AP Images/Reed Saxon, 26; Getty Images Inc./Elsa,
28; Getty Images Inc./Ethan Miller, 29; Getty Images Inc./Hulton Archive/
Express/David Cairns, 13; Getty Images Inc./Hulton Archive/Fox Photos, 11,
12; Getty Images Inc./Hulton Archive/Topical Press Agency, 8, 9; Getty Images
Inc./Quinn Rooney, 16; Getty Images Inc./Red Bull/Christian Pondella, 23
(bottom); Getty Images Inc./Rick Dole, 7; Getty Images Inc./Robert Cianflone,
25; Shutterstock/CTR Photos, cover; Shutterstock/Inc, 6; Shutterstock/Marcel
Jancovic, 21; Shutterstock/MISHELLA, 27 (right); Shutterstock/Randy
Miramontez, 27 (left)

Artistic Effects
Dreamstime/In-finity; Dreamstime/Michaelkovachev; iStockphoto/Michael Irwin;
iStockphoto/Russell Tate; Shutterstock/Els Jooren; Shutterstock/Fedorov Oleksiy;
Shutterstock/jgl247; Shutterstock/Marilyn Volan; Shutterstock/Pocike

Table of Contents

TEAR IT UP!

Forty dirt bike riders twist their throttle grips. Their bike engines roar. A flagman gives the 30-second warning. When the gate falls, the bikes blast off like rockets. Their rear tires shoot mud into the air, splattering the riders' colorful jerseys.

The riders zip to the first turn. They lean their bikes, dropping their right feet for balance. Some riders get stuck in the muck. Others fall and scramble to remount. Up ahead, the rest of the motocross racers disappear over jumps. It's a fierce fight to the finish line, and it's anyone's guess who the winner will be.

Motocross racers battle for the lead during the first turn. The first rider through claims the "hole shot" and can often keep a leading position.

Fast Fact: A rider may turn the bike sideways in midair to celebrate finishing a race. This move is called a whip.

BUILT TO TAKE A BEATING

Dirt bike riders must be tough inside and out. They need good concentration, balance, and physical strength. But that's not all. Riders also need super-strong machines.

Dirt bikes are specially built to travel fast on rough ground. They have lightweight parts and strong **suspension systems**. Knobby tires give them good grip. Whether they're on a racetrack or a steep mountain path, riders can depend on their machines.

The rear tire often sprays dirt into the air as it grips the surface.

suspension system — a system of springs and shock absorbers that absorbs the impact of riding over rough terrain

What it Takes to Ride

Motocross is one of the most physically demanding sports. Riders must stay in complete control of their speeding machines. Riders' hearts beat almost as fast as the hearts of pro mountain bikers and other pro athletes. Pro motocross racers must be at the top of their game for two 40-minute races in one day. They need endurance to keep from getting tired. To stay in top condition, riders often run, lift weights, and bicycle.

Riders also prepare mentally for competitions. Pro rider James Stewart said, "I try to focus on what I've done in training. Sometimes you get so nervous you just want to quit. But I think that's the thing that's gonna make you go even harder."

James Stewart

7

2 GETTING A GRIP

Today's dirt bike riders are treated to luxuries that early motorcyclists could only dream about. In the early 1900s, motorcycles looked like bicycles. These simple machines had little power. They were hard to handle on rough ground. But riders still pushed their bikes to the limit. They raced on bumpy gravel roads and around horse-racing tracks. They inched up hillsides in hill climb competitions. Over many years, the dirt bike took shape. But first, the earliest motorcyclists endured bumps, bruises, and countless wipeouts.

In the early 1900s, riders in hill climbs and other competitions wore no safety gear.

During World War I (1914–1918), soldiers used more than 20,000 motorcycles. Many soldiers rode motorcycles with attached sidecars to carry supplies. Motorcycles also were used as ambulances.

After the war, thousands of former soldiers wanted to buy their own motorcycles. In Britain, manufacturers struggled to keep up with the demand for about two years.

Many World War I soldiers delivered messages as dispatch riders.

MOTOCROSS IS BORN

Naturally, early riders wanted to prove their skills. These riders organized races. Most of the first races were long-distance endurance trials. Judges scored riders in parts of these races.

In 1924, members of a British motorcycle club wanted a race based on speed alone. Club members built a 2.5-mile (4-kilometer) cross-country track. Race participants would do laps around the track until they completed 50 miles (80 kilometers). Club members called their new race a "scramble." The 80 riders who took part bumped across the hilly course. Only 40 riders finished. Arthur Sparks, who was known as a skilled hill-climber, earned the win in just over two hours.

French riders quickly joined in on this new type of racing. They shortened the tracks and added jumps. Then they renamed the sport motocross, a combination of the words "motorcycle" and "cross-country."

Fast Fact: The 1924 scramble included a steep 200-yard (183-meter) hill called "Wild and Wooly." Most bikes didn't produce enough power to climb it. Spectators attached ropes to the motorcycles to pull some riders up the hill.

In a 1927 endurance trial, this steep hill was too much for many bike engines to handle.

● "REAL" DIRT BIKES AT LAST ●

Motocross exploded in Europe during the 1930s. In 1947, it went international with the first Motocross des Nations event.

In the 1950s, motocross tracks got more technical, and so did the bikes. Up to this point, motorcycles with heavy four-stroke engines were the norm. European manufacturers like CZ and Greeves began using lighter, more powerful two-stroke engines instead. With fewer parts, the two-stroke engine was more reliable and easier to maintain. Dirt bikes also had knobby tires by the mid-1950s, giving them better traction.

G. H. Jones flies through the air at an English motocross race in 1952.

In 1957, Husqvarna experimented with lightweight **alloy** parts for its Silver Arrow bike. With less weight, the bike was easier to handle. Within five years, alloy parts were part of Husqvarna's motocross bikes.

In the 1960s and 1970s, Japanese motorcycle manufacturers like Honda, Yamaha, and Suzuki revved the motocross world into high gear. Their bikes weighed less than 250 pounds (113 kilograms). Powerful two-stroke engines pushed these lightweight bikes to top speeds in record time. Japanese bikes also had strong suspension systems, large knobby tires, and wide handlebars. Most people consider these bikes to be the first true dirt bikes.

With nearly everyone on Japanese bikes in the 1970s, races were close and exciting.

alloy – a mixture of two or more metals

Motocross racers everywhere ordered truckloads of the sleek Japanese bikes. Before the 1960s, Americans had stood by while motocross gained popularity in Europe. But on their new Japanese bikes, Americans racked up championship titles alongside their European competitors. American motocross stars like Bob "Hurricane" Hannah and Mike "Too Tall" Bell led the way for future riders.

Across the United States, cheering motocross fans lined the racetracks. But they could see only the sections that were nearby. That changed when the first Supercross race was held in the Los Angeles Coliseum in 1972. Seated in a stadium, fans didn't have to miss a second of the track action.

Supercross tracks are shorter than motocross tracks, but their tight turns are a challenge for riders.

Bob Hannah takes first place in an international Supercross race in March 1977.

Fast Fact: Based on fan attendance, Supercross is second only to NASCAR racing in motorsport popularity.

LIGHTWEIGHT SPEED MACHINES

Dirt bikes of the 1970s were better than ever before. Even so, they are no match for today's bikes. Modern dirt bikes have high-tech suspension systems and powerful, **efficient** engines. Lightweight aluminum frames help jet them around racetracks and up hills.

When power from a dirt bike engine meets the rear wheel, dirt flies!

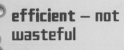

efficient – not wasteful

A dirt bike engine pumps out power like your heart pumps blood. The size of a dirt bike engine is measured in cubic centimeters, or ccs. The more ccs an engine has, the more powerful it is. Children often ride bikes with 50-cc to 85-cc engines. The 125-cc engine is popular with beginning adult riders. Pro American Motorcyclist Association (AMA) racers thunder across tracks on bikes with 250-cc or 450-cc engines.

After they were first invented, two-stroke engines became popular. These lightweight engines cranked out a lot of power. But two-strokes also burned a lot of gas. Eventually, people wanted bikes that used less fuel and caused less pollution. For these reasons, manufacturers began selling some dirt bikes with modern four-stroke engines in the early 2000s. Unlike four-strokes of the past, modern four-strokes are almost as powerful as two-strokes of a similar size. They are also lighter than earlier designs. Today, most AMA pro racing dirt bikes have four-stroke engines.

Fast Fact: Zero X is a high-performance electric dirt bike. It can zip from zero to 30 miles (48 kilometers) per hour in less than two seconds. It creates one-tenth the pollution of a gasoline-powered bike.

FRAME

A strong dirt bike frame is important for control and safety. In the 1990s, manufacturers built frames from aluminum instead of steel. Aluminum frames weighed less than steel, which helped the bikes quickly gain speed. But they were still strong enough to stand up to rough use.

SUSPENSION SYSTEM

Dirt bike riders rocket over jumps at high speeds. They need front and rear suspension systems to soften the landings. The first motorcycles had no suspension systems. By the late 1950s, suspension systems gave riders 3 to 4 inches (7.6 to 10 centimeters) of **wheel travel**. About 20 years later, dirt bikes had a single rear shock and a longer front **fork** for better shock absorption.

Modern dirt bikes have long-travel suspension systems. These systems provide about 12 inches (30 centimeters) of wheel travel at both the front and rear of the bikes. With them, riders can handle even the most brutal landing.

wheel travel – the distance between the highest point the suspension system can move to its lowest point

TRANSMISSION

Motorcycles have manual transmissions. Vehicles with these transmissions do not change gears automatically. Instead, the driver or rider must shift gears. Most dirt bikes have four to six gears. Riders shift through the gears as they speed up or slow down.

Long-travel suspension systems allow riders to go airborne with confidence.

fork — the part of a motorcycle that holds the front tire

WHEELS

Even the most powerful engine is worthless without the grip of the wheels. The rear wheel is slightly wider than the front wheel. With more ground contact, the rear tire can provide better grip.

The bumps on a dirt bike tire are called "knobbies," or treads. They help grip loose surfaces like sand and mud. Gaps between the treads keep mud from clumping up on the tire.

BRAKES

Strong brakes help riders slow down or stop in an instant. Without good stopping power, riders may slide off a track or slam into other riders. In the past, dirt bikes had drum brakes that provided little stopping power. Modern dirt bikes have hydraulic disc brakes that perform better.

FENDERS

Plastic fenders help block the mud that shoots off the tires. Keeping mud from blocking a rider's vision helps prevent wipeouts. For more clearance over obstacles, fenders sit 12 to 14 inches (30 to 36 centimeters) above the wheels.

Pro riders plaster their fenders with stickers from sponsors. In return, a sponsor gives a rider money and bike parts.

Weight:	200 to 250 pounds (91 to 113 kilograms)
Engine size:	50 ccs to 600 ccs; 250-cc and 450-cc engines are common for racing.
Top speed:	50 to 86 miles (80 to 138 kilometers) per hour
Transmission:	manual with 4 to 6 gears
Frame:	lightweight aluminum; frames weigh about 40 pounds (18 kilograms).
Tires:	have treads called knobbies; most tires are 18 to 21 inches (46 to 53 centimeters) around
Fenders:	plastic, with about 13 inches (33 centimeters) of clearance over the tires
Cost:	$2,000 to $10,000; pro bikes can cost as much as $60,000.

Riders sometimes use their brakes to adjust their position before landing.

21

Dirt bikes have their roots in motocross and Supercross. But these events only scrape the surface of the dirt biking world. Riders push their bikes — and their bravery — to the limit in many other daring events.

MOTOCROSS

The AMA sponsors both **amateur** and pro motocross races. Some pro racers are supported by bike manufacturers as "factory" riders. Riders who buy their own bikes and equipment are called privateers.

Each course is set up differently. Steep hills and various jumps are common. A step-up jump has a landing area that is higher than the take-off ramp. A double has two ramps separated by one gap, while a triple has three ramps separated by two gaps. Most racers can jump 70 to 100 feet (21 to 30 meters) in length. They may clear a double or a triple with one takeoff.

amateur – describes a race in which riders are competing for fun rather than to make a living

On a steep hill, racers must keep up their speed. But with too much power, the front tire can lift.

Fast Fact: Australian Robbie Maddison set a new world record in 2007 by jumping 322 feet (98 meters). That's as long as three blue whales!

Up to 40 motocross riders compete in two races called motos. Amateur motos last 10 to 30 minutes each. Professionals race for 30 minutes plus two laps in each moto. Riders receive points based on their finishes. The riders in the top placings receive the most points. After both motos, the points from each one are combined. The rider with the most points wins the event.

⚙ SUPERCROSS ⚙

Supercross tracks can take more than 800 tons (726 metric tons) of dirt to build. Long rows of small bumps called whoops are a big part of the courses.

Riders in pro AMA Supercross races qualify by competing in two heats. The top nine racers in each heat advance to the main event. Riders who don't qualify take part in a "last-chance" event. The first- and second-place finishers from this race ride in the main event as well. In the main event, riders complete 20 laps in the 450 Premier class. For the 250 Lites class, racers complete 15 laps.

Riders shift their weight to the back of their bikes to help avoid crashes over whoops.

Fast Fact: The AMA sponsors amateur and pro motocross series for women as well as men. The Women's Motocross Association (WMA) formed in 2004.

25

FREESTYLE MOTOCROSS

Freestyle motocross (FMX) riders perform wild stunts in midair. These daredevils fly off 10- to 15-foot (3- to 4.6-meter) ramps. They often soar more than four stories in the air. The sport's intensity has made it one of the fastest growing extreme sports. The X Games and the events of the Dew Action Sports Tour make up the major competitions. Riders are judged on the difficulty and style of their tricks over a series of jumps.

Never satisfied, pro FMX riders are constantly creating spectacular new tricks. Carey Hart is well known for inventing the Hart attack in the late 1990s. In 2006, Travis Pastrana became the first rider to land a double backflip at a competition. The next year, Kyle Loza thrilled fans with a new trick that he named the volt. Both Pastrana and Loza earned a gold medal for these wild tricks at the X Games.

Kyle Loza performed the volt during his first X Games appearance.

FMX
Trick Glossary

backflip 360: The rider performs a backflip while spinning in a complete circle.

can can: The rider takes one foot off the peg, swings it over the seat, and moves it back again before landing.

cliffhanger: The rider lets the bike drop in the air and catches the handlebars with his feet.

Hart attack: The rider grabs onto the seat while kicking both legs straight up in the air.

kiss of death: The rider does a handstand above the bike, keeping the elbows bent and his head close to the front fender.

one-footer: The rider kicks out one foot.

one-hander: The rider sticks one hand straight out.

Superman backflip: The rider does a backflip while stretching out his legs behind him.

Superman seat grab: The rider takes both hands off the handlebars and both feet off the pegs. He then grabs the back of the seat with both hands and stretches his feet out behind him.

volt: The rider gets off the bike, spins in a full circle, and gets back on before landing.

Hart attack

cliffhanger

Dirt bike riding is more than just motocross, Supercross, or freestyle. Arenacross races are similar to Supercross races, except they are held in smaller arenas. Long-distance enduro racers wind through dusty trails for hundreds of miles. In 2008, Robby Bell, Kendall Norman, and Johnny Campbell won the 631-mile (1,015-kilometer) Baja 1000. It took them more than 12 hours!

In the X Games Step-up event, riders must clear a bar set 25 to 29 feet (7.6 to 8.8 meters) above the lip of a jump. If a rider knocks down the bar, he has one more chance before being **eliminated**. After each round, the bar is raised. The last rider remaining is crowned the Step-up champion.

Jeremy Carter soars over the bar during the Step-up event in 2002.

eliminated – to be removed from a competition by a defeat

28

REACHING NEW HEIGHTS

Dirt biking is all about speed, style, and raw talent. No matter the event, riders push their sport to new heights. Motocross and Supercross champion Mike Bell said, "It is almost an unreal experience to take the checkered flag and win a race in front of 80,000 spectators. Honestly, words can't give that moment justice. Winning never gets old."

Fast Fact: "Godfather of Freestyle" Mike Metzger holds the distance record for the longest backflip. In 2006, he backflipped 125 feet (38 meters) over the fountains at Caesar's Palace in Las Vegas.

GLOSSARY

alloy (AL-oy) — a mixture of two or more metals

amateur (A-muh-chuhr) — describes an activity in which people compete for pleasure rather than for money

clearance (KLEER-uhns) — the space between two objects; dirt bikes have a great deal of clearance between the front wheel and the front fender to travel over obstacles.

cubic centimeter (KYOO-bik SEN-tuh-mee-tuhr) — a unit that measures the size of a motorcycle engine; this unit is abbreviated "cc."

disc brake (DISK BRAYK) — a type of brake that uses a metal disc to stop the wheel from spinning

drum brake (DRUM BRAYK) — a type of brake that uses brake shoes to stop the wheel from spinning

efficient (uh-FI-shuhnt) — not wasteful of time or energy

eliminated (i-LIM-uh-nay-ted) — to be removed from a competition by a defeat

fork (FORK) — the part of a motorcycle that holds the front tire

hydraulic (hye-DRAW-lik) — having to do with a system powered by fluid forced through pipes or chambers

moto (MOH-toh) — a single motocross race; each motocross event includes two motos.

suspension system (suh-SPEN-shuhn SISS-tuhm) — a system of springs and shock absorbers that absorbs the impact of riding over rough ground

tread (TRED) — a series of bumps and deep grooves on a tire

wheel travel (WEEL TRAV-uhl) — the distance between the highest point the suspension system can move to its lowest point

READ MORE

Dayton, Connor. *Dirt Bikes.* Motorcycles: Made for Speed! New York: PowerKids Press, 2007.

Oxlade, Chris. *Motorcycles Inside and Out.* Machines Inside Out. New York: PowerKids Press, 2009.

Tieck, Sarah. *Dirt Bikes.* Amazing Vehicles. Edina, Minn.: ABDO, 2009.

Young, Jeff C. *Motorcycles: The Ins and Outs of Superbikes, Choppers, and Other Motorcycles.* RPM. Mankato, Minn.: Capstone Press, 2010.

INTERNET SITES

FactHound offers a safe, fun way to find Internet sites related to this book. All of the sites on FactHound have been researched by our staff.

Here's all you do:

Visit *www.facthound.com*

FactHound will fetch the best sites for you!

Index